D1792956

All the Best

WE ONLY WEEP IN DREAMS

WE ONLY WEEP IN DREAMS

Timothy Muller

Black Bishop Press

Copyright © 2010 by Timothy Muller

All rights reserved. No part of this book may be reproduced or transmitted in any form or by any means without the written permission of the author, except for brief excerpts for use by a reviewer.

Manufactured in the United States of America

ISBN 978-0-615-38644-7

Library of Congress Control Number: 2010910321

Cover Photo by Ricardo Andre Frantz
Sculpture: Mary Magdalene by Gregor Erhart

Black Bishop Press
DeWitt, New York

CONTENTS

ON THE STREET	1
SAY GOOD-BYE	3
AMONG TALL RUINED HOMES	5
HER DEFENSE	6
NOT IN SPRING	7
CLODIA AT TRAIL	11
THE SORROW OF HELEN.	13
CLEOPATRA'S COMPLAINT	14
MARY MAGDALENE AT THE CROSS	16
THE MIRRORED CHEST	19
SUCH A HEAVY SPELL	21
HER CONFESSION	23
SHE THINKS OF HER DEATH	25
CLODIA IN THE FORUM	29
THE LADIES OF THE NIGHT	31
THE QUEENS OF THE DEAD	32
THE GEISHA	33
OVER THE OLD STREETS	34
SHE DREAMS OF TRUE LOVE	37
FROM COLD TO COLD	38
PURGATORY	39
HER HEART	40
THE ANOINTING OF THE SICK.	41
ON SUMMER NIGHTS	43
MY BODY	44
THE DOMINATRIX	45
HER MOTHER'S PRAYER	46

THOUGH YOUR LIFE HAS BEEN BROKEN	49
MAYBE SHE WAS ONE	50
MY SWEETNESS AND MY BLAME	52
TONIGHT TO YOU	53
THE FIRE	57
IN THE DARKNESS	59
WHEN SHE RETURNS	61
A SECOND CAREER	62
LORD HER BEAUTY'S FADED	63
WATCHMEN OF THE YEARS	64
MAYBE I ONLY DREAMED	65
MAGDALA, 1 BC	67
YOSHIWARA	68

1

ON THE STREET

The flakes of snow are not to hide her,
Gaudily dressed and very pale,
Half a woman, and half a child,
Flagrant, on the street for sale.

Her face is the face of a manikin,
Her eyes wooden and hollow;
But beautiful and gentle, her hands
Might lift a swallow.

We too have hands,
Hands that might hold or heal;
Faces that may open in time,
Or fail to, and congeal.

The cold is deepening;
The snow is settling over all.
She has nothing to tie the heart to;
Her share in life is small.

The human mind is small;
It cannot ascertain
Why there should be such beauty
Mingled so with pain.

2

SAY GOOD-BYE

The sky's so many gems of light
Shine over oaks and elms tonight;
The wind is stirring all the trees;
But then, you never notice these.

Through rented rooms with smutty sheets
That stretch beneath on broken streets,
Through bars and alcoholic haze,
You bundle up your nights and days.

You must have once like any child
Run up and down, carefree and wild
On lawns beneath red darkening skies;
You must have watched the fireflies.

You must have heaped up leaves in play
Once on some October day,
And not then seen whatever bend
Would turn and take you towards this end.

How could you like other girls
With limber limbs and subtle curls
Have known that you would come to this:
To sell your love but still not kiss.

Someone must have taught you how
To say good-bye when you were small,
So say good-bye forever now
To the supple heart you can't recall.

They keep you up so late at night,
So say good-bye to the early light,
Good-bye to the dew and moonlit dawns,
Good-bye to the bright red leaves and the lawns.

Then say good-bye to the fireflies
That lit the night in your widening eyes,
Once long ago beneath the stars,
Above the rented rooms and bars.

3

AMONG TALL RUINED HOMES

She sells herself in a dying part of town,
Loitering among tall ruined homes;
Alone, night after night she roams
These streets since long ago she fell far down;

Fell down like the unburied and the poor,
Lotted to linger on and on
Beside the sorrowful Acheron,
To linger a hundred years by that dark shore.

Under what ancient order will she be
Here on these streets that cry out sorrow
Beneath the lamplight again tomorrow?
What age-old dispensation, what divine decree?

4

HER DEFENSE

I do not dread to yield to their desires;
I have no need to stoop down or condescend;
I bring into the soft sheen and shimmering light
That night permits the changing shapes of cravings
That go creeping in the cellarage of the mind
And ghost-like fret the lonely lost in sleep.

I have heard each harsh word they spoke against me,
And Sir, I sidestep pitfalls as well as you,
And I have kept faith with this world's demands;
And when the morning comes, and Sir, it does,
And all the dew-drenched grass is green again
Then you can see me saunter down the street
And watch my haughty rhythms and bright bracelets,
And see that children come to me that that shy from you.

5

NOT IN SPRING

Not in spring will I think of her –
Those giddy fragrant days –
And not in summertime,
Nor in autumn's brilliant blaze.

But I will think of her
On some November day
When the wind blows leafless trees
In fields turned ashen gray.

6

CLODIA AT TRIAL

Then, when the proconsul was done,
And all that Clodia had ever been,
So full of hunger, but then so proud,
Was placed before the court and crowd;
Where every intricate desire
Incited laughter, and the entire
Roman elite had watched her face
Emotionless in her disgrace,
What happened then? Did Clodia mend
Her way of life before the end?

The old historians scarcely dwell
On Clodia. Still there's this to tell:
Time made her more inclined to drift;
In time she only seemed to shift
From love to love and haunt to haunt,
Until aging and growing gaunt
She sometimes lurked in alleyways –
Sad mockery of her early days.

Though some of all who'd gathered there
Declined to taunt or jeer; since they
Whose lips had pressed against her hair
Found a bitter-sweetness there;
They'd found with her a kind of home,
Who'd found it nowhere else in Rome.

7

THE SORROW OF HELEN

The winds of Argos bring relief
To Helen bored with Trojan strife;
Her consolation though is brief;
The queen, her sister, lost her life.

So she thinks of how to show her grief,
Of emblems long since custom-bound –
Wine and milk, honey and hair –
To place upon the burial mound.

She puzzles long on the locks of hair;
She thinks a little from the tips she'll spare;
She thinks one honeyed strand's enough,
But guarding her beauty, but guarding our love.

8

CLEOPATRA'S COMPLAINT

The pitfalls here in Egypt hold more than adders.
We are subtle here. The Romans, clumsy and coarse,
Sink in the quicksands of this our eastern life.
This is the land of mirage, you can see what you wish;
Here you must distinguish, you must discern.
And I learned early to play with light and scents,
To mingle odors on the desert air
And frame my face among the torches in the halls
And float the lanterns on the Nile, and such a show!
But I've grown tired; I long to leave this heat
And go to the dark painted tombs, the house of the gods;
I will linger in the anterooms of hell;
I will listen to the dead make their faint pleas,
And when at last I am able to speak freely
I will make my confession and say that my deception
Was nothing worse than the deception of the gods
      themselves.

My heart, my mother, weighs the weight of a feather
And Osiris will demand no more, and I will go
And walk in his bright emerald light forever.
But now I wonder what more must I do;
How many mouths are hungering for my breasts?
How many blood-stained Caesars troop from Rome?

9

MARY MAGDALENE AT THE CROSS

Stark against the darkening olive sky,
The soldiers raise the sallow carcass high,
And there it bleeds for all the world in vain;
It lingers on and on in utmost pain.

O why should my Lord Jesus suffer so?
If all this agony could cast its spell
And lighten this world's dark citadel,
Then such as I'd have saved it long ago.

What else could goad me on from lane to lane
Except for hope for balm to soothe the pain,
That pain from guilt that always filled my cup,
That guilt the world long since had gathered up?

10

THE MIRRORED CHEST

In front of the mirrored chest
She sits and stares. This time
Is not the first nor last.
She hears some clock's late chime.
She looks for the beauty there,
The beauty all others see:
The dark cascading hair
And the great audacious eyes
Which serve her now so ill,
And faint around the lips
A rim of blue from a chill;
And then the nightgown slips,
Baring there the white
And scented flesh from hips
To throat.   Recessed at night
In rooms what memories come:
The dumbstruck looks of men
Like children overcome
When wading out and then
Beyond their depths in pools.

Her body though to her
Is carrion wracked with ills
Which God may now inter,
Now, or when He wills.

She rises up to latch
The door; we know that there
Is none to overmatch
The voice indicting her;
Outside old crows are perched in ranks
And unclean rivers plumb their banks.

11

SUCH A HEAVY SPELL

When sometimes at a loss to speak
Of what I want, I think to tell
How in the hollow of her cheek
The fever of the night grows cool;

And I might praise the skin and the lips,
And I could tell how the slender chest
Undulates from throat to hips
And bears the burden of the breast;

And tell of the tall head and the hair
And all the rest; and I might do well
Granted all the beauty there,
But what I want, I cannot tell;

Because, with movements full of grace,
After all her tears are spilt,
She plies the blush to hide the face,
That hides the sorrow and hides the guilt,

And then I undertake to tell
The bravery of her heart,
When under such a heavy spell
Will and strength to speak depart.

12

HER CONFESSION

Forgive me Father, for I have sinned;
By now you know me well enough –
I've broken every law of love;
Those laws that no one may rescind.

The moon's not mine, not mine the night
When the city hums its midnight song;
But it's there that I feel that I belong
And there it's hard to feel contrite.

I'm sure there're those whose love is strong
Who lying down to bed at night
Feel time and again their love ignite;
And if that's true, may they love long.

Maybe I've seen them by the sea
Walking slowly hand in hand
On the lighted beach while far from land
Dark ships pass over the dark sea.

Father, my stretch of days has thinned;
I've broken every law of love,
Those laws we've often spoken of;
Forgive me Father, for I have sinned.

13

SHE THINKS OF HER DEATH

I wake at night afraid of dying,
And then sometimes I pray;
But death, my death, I know for certain
Will come some sudden day.

And on that day there'll be few mourners
For fear of their good name;
I think of some who would want to come,
Who'll stay away for shame.

So find a plain and simple casket
Where at last I'm laid;
Prepare me for the clasp of God,
For whom that bed is made.

I think it best there be no candles,
Or let them not be lit;
I stumbled all through darkness, and how
Will light then benefit?

Roses and lilies are best forgotten,
Blue violets prone to wilt;
Flowers for solemnity and love,
But where's the flower for guilt?

Then make me up with blush and lipstick
Bright and florid for a whore,
And on a little headstone set this:
She might have died before.

14

CLODIA IN THE FORUM

What feelings stirred in Clodia on that day
She came to court, then lost and went away?
What was it that Clodia felt before she walked
Out to the Forum where the people talked
And taunted in the stillness of the spring air,
And marble tier upon tier and stair on stair?
The ache that urged her through the streets of Rome,
They'd put on trial. They'd opened up her home –
The torch-lit passageways and scented rooms
Lush with sea-breeze and Syrian perfumes –
And brought to mind each new revealing eye,
Each desperate brave embrace and harsh goodbye,
And every restless night and drowsing day.

Maybe she felt nothing, or went away
Ashamed; maybe she felt some sadness stir;
How can we know? We only know of her
As she appeared before the court. We sense
The dark, rich, Roman blood along the veins,
Imagine the cool eyes, the impassive face;

We sense her heightened mediterranean grace;
And then she passes out of sight, she's gone,
And all her luck and drifting days seem done;
And what she felt? that we can never know;
The Forum's in ruin; all this was long ago.

15

THE LADIES OF THE NIGHT

The ladies of the night watch closely in silence;
Their faces are still and their eyes are still;
Their knowledge is the knowledge of the streets;
They know the secrets and know the secret places.
The women of the night weep rarely.
Their laughter is a forced laughter;
Their laughter is sadder than tears.
They kiss rarely, the women of the streets,
But then they kiss deep and never let go.
The name of the Lord is on their lips –
Their prayers are innumerable;
Even their curses are prayers.
The ladies of the dark wear the dark scents of musk and myrrh;
They wear the scents of the rose and Spanish jasmine,
Of lilac and Indian sandalwood;
For these are gathered odors from over the whole earth.

16

THE QUEENS OF THE DEAD

Those women at their age-old trade tonight
Summon and beckon, linger and delay;
They gather underneath the yellow light
And loiter there, but then they drift away
Into a night whose darkness they belie.
Did one there bear a child then watch her die?
And did another dearly love the sea?
Or did the third conceal a shameful flaw
And somehow think that here she might be free?
And was it some like scene the traveler saw
In the amber gloom beyond the blood filled pit,
That afterworld no sun had ever lit,
Hovering there in the vapor and the mist
The souls bereft of strength, stricken with thirst
For the bright light and then the dark rich blood,
Those queens forever drifting among the dead?

17

THE GEISHA

Autumn is all but over now;
A drifting chill creeps somehow
Along the floor. I try to recall
How often winter's followed fall
Since my own mother turned her face
Ashamed against the old stone wall
And I heard the silver coins fall,
And they brought me to this strange land,
Here where I wonder if I understand
That golden world beyond the gate,
That world they speak so often of.
This chill has chilled me to the marrow,
And I should go, or so it seems;
As I have a face for love,
So I have a face for sorrow;
We only weep in dreams.

18

OVER THE OLD STREETS

The numberless harlots were flowing like a stream
Over the old, old streets stretching on,
The streets of Ur, Rome and Babylon,
My wandering sisters, in a dream.

Then came their vagrant mothers, bought and sold;
I heard them cry out, "We will die tomorrow,
And who then will carry this world's age-old sorrow?"
Their slender bodies growing old.

Among the small dwelling places of the dead,
On the cobblestone streets roamed orphaned daughters;
Under a setting sun, they drifted like the waters;
They were hungry and unfed.

19

SHE DREAMS OF TRUE LOVE

Although she trades her love away,
She dreams of love that perseveres;
She dreams of a love that outlasts the day,
Of love that echoes down the years.

And lying down to bed at night,
She thinks of lace and silver things,
Of marriage in rose rouge and white,
Of two hands linked with two gold rings.

These daydreams keep tomorrow at bay,
Tomorrow and all the days to come,
The drifting, tawdry days, the way
The years pile up, and what she has become.

20

FROM COLD TO COLD

She thinks that for a heart in love,
That nothing thwarts its grace and ease,
And thinks it's like a flight of gulls
When the gulls drift over the seas.

But still inside herself she fathoms
There's little fondness to impart –
Permits no feigning of affection,
Concedes her stubborn heart;

Though living so, it's hard to step,
Hard to bend and hard to hold,
And flight's the flight of northern geese
That drift from cold to cold.

21

PURGATORY

Because her beauty's rare,
And since she leaves at dark,
The neighbors are prone to talk
And make some snide remark.

But take away the pain
And heal for good the sore
That sometimes heals a little
But always festers more;

Then the beauty of her form
When she passes heaven's door
Will seem the distillation
Of sweetness at the core.

22

HER HEART

If you had held her by the wrist
You would have felt heart insist
That it was not a beating drum,
Summoning battles still to come,
And no metallic recurring chime,
Tabulating hollow time;
Her heart was not an echoing gong,
Sounding out an ancient wrong,
But some precarious thing of flesh and blood,
Before before she took her lovers on to bed.

23

THE ANOINTING OF THE SICK

They bring in the priest with his crucifix,
His black-bound book for a psalm;
Here are white candles on candlesticks,
The oil, the cruse, and the palm.

They hope that the oil will prove potent;
They hope that the body may heal,
At least that the spirit be strengthened,
Should the blood begin to congeal.

And though the illness itself is dire,
The sick may yet grow strong;
The strong can be quick to surrender,
And the frail may linger long.

But what of her whom the rest have forgotten,
Who lies in a different bed,
In some last extremity of love,
Its drama and its dread?

The oil must prove more potent
When only the mind is ill;
The blood may be slow to recover;
But the heart is slower still.

And the priest is not likely to come
With his dreary mumble of a psalm,
The two tall candles and candlesticks,
The oil, the cruse, and the palm.

24

ON SUMMER NIGHTS

On summer nights when the cricket sings,
It's easy to sense the drift of things.
The breaking waves and the beach tonight
Are fading now in the lessening light.

A seagull high in its stony home
Is watching out over the ocean's foam –
Watching its mate return with food –
And soon they'll feed their hungry brood.

Above, the constellations arc
Around the North Star through the dark,
And there's a strange decorum kept
While we below have watched or slept.

On summer nights while the cricket sings,
It's hard not to hear the drift of things;
So faithfulness is my refrain
That answers my despair and pain.

25

MY BODY

My body's given up to others;
But sometimes I must keep –
Although it's held in slight esteem –
My body for myself alone,
If only just to sleep,
If only just to dream.

26

THE DOMINATRIX

Sometimes at home alone in bed
The past comes back with all its dread:
The drafty house and silent rooms
When even the walls seemed ill at ease;
Outdoors the wind and apple trees.

The sudden rage that split the air;
The body beaten in despair;
The naked flesh and searing pain
And echoing down the hall the screams
And sobs. These memories come in dreams.

But when these dreams fade out at dawn
The bruises and the pain are gone;
Her body's lovely, lush and sweet,
The body men kneel down to kiss,
The flesh they cherish and they caress.

27

HER MOTHER'S PRAYER

A girl lingers on a stretch of broken street,
While her mother prays to Mary's statuette
For things not done, and done to her regret,
And prays her daughter leave that indiscreet
And drifting life – that she come home tonight,
Come home to where it's light and where it's warm;
And on and on she pleads with the calm form
Of the Virgin robed in blue beneath the light.

And Mother Mary knows that in the end
They all come home, but what answer might she make?
For she knows too the sorrow of children who take
To streets not foreseen, roads that quickly bend,
Some lane to sudden loss, some thoroughfare,
Long and winding, hard and hard to bear.

28

THOUGH YOUR LIFE HAS BEEN BROKEN

Though your life has been broken down to the core
And you are unwelcome in the churches and the temples,
Do not therefore conclude that God has abandoned you;
It may be that it is you God loves most of all;
Perhaps it is you who concerns God most;
It is you to whom God has given beauty
And however you misuse or misspend it
Still it is yours; as when upon some April morning
You saunter down the street in your ethereal youth
And so gather gazes from every longing or envious eye.

29

MAYBE SHE WAS ONE

His courage was nothing much, but still it took
It all and all his will to turn and look
Into her blue eyes and ask her face to face,
And thus confirm depravity and disgrace.

She looked away and smiled at his distress;
But then said "yes," she said she would, "of course,"
And then began to step out of her dress,
Flooding the room with sudden nakedness.

In ancient Rome they had an adage then:
"To me there's nothing human that's alien;"
"Nihil … alienum" some poet sang;
How easily it goes in the old tongue.

How easily it flows – easily slips
Past a writer's pen or a scholar's lips;
Brave words of poets and of learned men,
But to how many do these fine words pertain?

Though maybe she was one, was really one,
To whom no human thing was alien;
In any case, she smiled and answered "yes,"
And then began to step out of her dress.

30

MY SWEETNESS AND MY BLAME

There are some that shun me when it's light
Who come and look for me at night;
They find me on this lamplit street,
And then, like children, they hold me tight.

There are strange attendants on these nights:
Streetlamps, dark trees and lurking heights;
There's Jesus on a lighted cross,
The moon and I, high silhouettes.

Things that sunlight shows too stark
Soften and glisten in the dark:
Sheer silk over a bruised thigh;
Kissed garters over the hip's arc.

Like fragrances of musk and myrrh
Or like some amber, rich liqueur,
The source and essence are the same
Of all my sweetness and my blame.

31

TONIGHT TO YOU

No one should have to walk these streets
As you and I on troubled nights.
You're here for someone's dark mistake
Made long ago, and I for the ache.

We walk these streets at night alone
Because tonight you'll be my own;
Because for money I may borrow
My own sweet love until tommorrow.

These streets are filled with hate; they're dark,
And only the streetlamps over the park
Shed light where the horse and soldier stand
On guard in this barbaric land.

We lie here hungry; such hunger brings
Rash acts, regrets – so many things;
But I must be glad for all this too,
That brought me, love, tonight to you.

32

THE FIRE

When fire in France lit up the dark
To burn to death St. Joan of Arc,
She fixed on Christ a steady gaze
Till overcome in the bounding blaze.

In somber Spain St. John of the Cross,
Who knew God's glory and knew the loss,
Learned of God's fierce conflagration
In the flame of his purgation.

And once on a black Italian night
The peasants claimed the woods grew bright
When St. Francis met St. Clare;
They'd lit the incandescence there.

All saints who burn in God's great flame
Are free from anger, sorrow and shame;
But I burn too, I burn at night,
With no repose and no respite.

A fire is yellow, orange and blue;
It flares in reds of every hue;
O when shall I lie still and free
Of all the heat that burns in me?

33

IN THE DARKNESS

When some young shephard come from Galilee
Had left his flock beside its silver sea
And made his way to Mary Magdalene
To share her common bed and share her sin,
Did he, trembling in the half-light there,
Reach out to touch her hips or touch her hair,
Amazed, sense so much life beneath the skin?
Beside her there, was there uncommon heat,
And did her body seem to burn?
Did he feel and cold and dull in turn?
Did her heart beat with a quicker beat,
And did her skin flush warm until it gleamed?
Did her soul's youth shine through so that it seemed
To keep her young through strange long years,
The roads, the cross, the empty tomb and tears?

Such things are not set down and now there's none
To tell. Two thousand years have come and gone,
And yet the pilgrims climb the steep high hill
Near Vezelay and there adore her still.
She stands somewhere gaunt, ragged and unshod;

She stands not far from the Mother of God
In the statuary at Rennes le Chataeux
Robed in resplendent reds, soft golds, and blue;
And still they come, come all who will;
They come; so many long to touch her still.

34

WHEN SHE RETURNS

Ah, lonely lamplit girl, go home;
Leave these streets you're prone to roam;
Go inside your little room,
Light a candle and lift the gloom,
The gloom that shrouds the Virgin there
Silent in the vibrant air;
Then gaze into the face of Mary
And on your knees now say your Ave;
But think how fortunate they are
Those children never straying far
Who when they feel the burning stir
Consecrate that fire to her.

35

A SECOND CAREER

When the faint lines and heavy drooping breast
And time convinced her she was past her best,
And men preferred the younger girls, still taut,
Still firm, she felt neither envy nor regret,
Since she knew well how young girls age so soon;
Instead she found a tonier part of town
And there stripped off the cheap and slinky clothes
And bought expensive ones, dark tones and silk hose;
Then dressed in rich fabrics she left the store,
Aware that in this city nothing more
Was needed; now that her hemline's past her thigh
There are ten thousand trades for her to ply.

36

LORD HER BEAUTY'S FADED

Lord, her beauty's faded, all but gone;
And the stir that trailed about her everywhere
Is now recessed deep into hollow time;
But give to others tears for anodyne.

From vain regret she reaps no benefit;
The spare and unaccompanied days to come
Are like the chill of wind through winter pine,
Or like the soldier's dawn before the fires are lit.

37

WATCHMEN OF THE YEARS

If there were watchmen of the years,
Those whose only business were to note the passing time,
To keep a tally of what's gone, of all that disappears,
To remember always what will not return,
Then, like those watchmen of the years,
I, who look on as one looks seaward
From ruined harbors or old abandoned piers,
Could say that I have trade enough,
If there were watchmen of the years.

38

MAYBE I ONLY DREAMED

Maybe I never walked those streets at all
And never did disrobe in the dark chill,
Times out of mind far down some empty hall,
My body sometimes pleased against my will.

And it could be that I never ached with cold
Underneath a red December sky,
And that my love was never bought or sold,
That I had nothing to sell or they to buy.

And is it true as the old masters claim
That all around are things that only seem –
Only empty forms? that we only came
To earth to sleep, we only came to dream?

Maybe all these things never did occur;
I never lurked alone in alleyways,
A shadow, something nearly sinister,
Haunted and hunted, dark beneath the eyes.

Maybe only diverted like a stream,
For a little while I dreamed an alien dream
Of an ageing woman who came to comprehend
The dark. My troubled dreaming soon must end.

39

MAGDALA, 1 BC

Then, when you come at night to that last lane,
You'll find a little girl alone in pain,
Inside the doorway of a rented room;
Her hair is dark, her checks are a peach bloom.

It's here her mother keeps a bed to share
For only some little money here and there,
With tradesmen, Roman soldiers, or young clerk
Or hooded Pharisee slinking after dark.

And Mary too in time will sell her love,
Because she'll feel it is all she'll ever have;
For now the wide black eyes take in,
With evening's light, the sorrow and sin.

How can she know that now the Magi stir,
Freighted with gold and frankincense and myrrh,
That even now they cross white windblown drifts
Of desert, that now nearby they set down gifts,

And kneel to all heaven's glory and awe,
Now sleeping as an infant on a bed of straw?

40

YOSHIWARA

You who would judge me, come to Yoshiwara.
Here the moat that circumscribes our virtue
And our vice reflects the colored lanterns,
And in that light the blossoms drift forever;
And here the red and purple silken robes
And studded golden hairpins sway and glitter
Among the incense and the candles' light.
Long years ago I came against my will;
It's here I learned to play the samisen
And learned to paint my face as white as chalk;
Here I learned my slow and patterned dance
And how to sing my frail seductive songs,
All from the obasan reciting now
The rites of death to mock the Shin-Shu priest,
Come to select his consort for the night.
Here I have heard nothing of great Buddha,
Lord of Compassion, or of Nirvana
Where all is banished into the eternal;

But when I bow to his image on my shelf
I think it's he who turns the moon and stars
And turns this drifting world from day to day.
And when late at night I hear the watchmen sound
The wooden blocks, and then the gates are locked
On this our timeless world, I think that here
Our vice and virtue are of one single strand.
Do not judge me then by some alien code,
My only schooling was in forms of love.